What W Negro Leagues?

by Varian Johnson

illustrated by Stephen Marchesi

Penguin Workshop

To the VCFA faculty, for reminding me
how much I love nonfiction—VJ

For Bill Mantlo, who always stood up
for the underdog—SM

PENGUIN WORKSHOP
An Imprint of Penguin Random House LLC, New York

Visit us online at www.penguinrandomhouse.com.

Library of Congress Cataloging-in-Publication Data is available upon request.

ISBN 9781524789985 (paperback)   10 9 8 7 6 5 4 3 2 1
ISBN 9781524789992 (library binding)   10 9 8 7 6 5 4 3 2 1

Contents

What Were the Negro Leagues?

September 8, 1942: On a warm Tuesday, twenty thousand fans filed into the bleachers of Griffith Stadium in Washington, DC, to watch the first game in the World Series. The best-of-seven-game series was sure to be an exciting spectacle, with the top two teams competing against each other. The series featured some of the biggest baseball stars of the day—many of whom were later inducted into the Baseball Hall of Fame.

But this game didn't include big names, such as Joe DiMaggio or Ted Williams. Nor were Major League Baseball (MLB) teams, such as the Boston Red Sox or the New York Yankees, battling against each other.

That's because this was the Negro League World Series. All of the players on both teams—

the Homestead Grays and the Kansas City Monarchs—were black.

(Before the 1960s, *Negro* was considered the polite way to refer to black people. Today, that is no longer the case.)

In 1942, not one major-league team had any African Americans on its roster. Why? White players refused to play with black teammates. So none were hired.

Black baseball players were just as good as or better than white players from the major leagues. The 1942 Negro League World Series featured seven future Hall of Famers, including Leroy Robert "Satchel" Paige. He was perhaps the best pitcher in Negro League

Leroy Robert "Satchel" Paige

history. Also, Josh Gibson. He was one of the most powerful hitters ever. Josh Gibson was so good at belting out home runs, many people called him "the Black Babe Ruth," though fans who saw both players often called Ruth "the White Josh Gibson."

Josh Gibson

The first few innings of the opening game of the 1942 Negro World Series were close. Neither team was able to score. But in the fourth inning, two Homestead Gray players finally made it on base. Then came Gibson, six feet one and weighing over two hundred pounds. Satchel Paige stood across from him at the pitcher's mound.

The best against the best.

Paige wound up and pitched the ball. It went

flying across the infield. Gibson swung, and
with a crack, the bat connected. The ball flew
far and high . . . but not far enough and not high
enough. The ball was caught at center field.

Gibson was out.

There would be no home runs for Gibson or the Homestead Grays that day. The Kansas City

Monarchs won the first game 8–0.

In the second game, Paige and Gibson faced each other again. Some said that Satchel Paige deliberately walked two players, loading the bases, just so he could pitch against Josh Gibson. Former Monarchs player and manager John "Buck" O'Neil even claimed Paige taunted Gibson before striking the slugger out with a "one-hundred-and-five-mile [an-hour] fastball."

Although Paige probably didn't walk two players on purpose, the series became a classic. Thanks to Paige, Gibson, and others, over sixty thousand fans attended the World Series!

None of the players could know that Negro League baseball was almost at its peak. Big changes would soon come to baseball. And even though these changes led to the end of the Negro Leagues, its legacy would continue to live on and inspire today's fans.

CHAPTER 1
The Beginning of Baseball

Standardized baseball in America began in 1845. That's when the first written rules were created for the New York Knickerbockers baseball team. Before this, many ballplayers played other "bat and ball" games, like cricket, a game from England. By the time the Civil War began in 1861, thousands of people were playing baseball all across the country. The war even increased

the sport's popularity. Whenever soldiers got the chance, they would play baseball for fun and teach one another about the game.

As more and more people became baseball fans and watched local games, some teams decided to turn professional. In 1869, the Cincinnati Red Stockings became the first baseball club to pay its team members for playing. The Red Stockings traveled around the country, sometimes bringing in crowds of twenty thousand people.

The Cincinnati Red Stockings

As news of the Red Stockings' success spread, more teams began to turn professional. In time, these teams began to work together to form *organized* leagues, with standard pay for their players and set schedules for their teams. Eventually, the two main baseball leagues—the National League and the American League—came to be known as Major League Baseball, or the majors.

The end of the Civil War led to the end of slavery. Black people began to play popular sports, like baseball, that before had been reserved for whites. But many white people believed that the two races should stay separated from each other. (This is called segregation.) They shouldn't be playing baseball with each other. But maybe there was also another reason. Perhaps white players did not want to be embarrassed by being struck out by a black pitcher or having a black player score a home run on them.

John "Bud" Fowler

Although many baseball clubs were racist, some black players did make it onto white baseball teams. One was John "Bud" Fowler. Born in 1858 in New York, Fowler became a professional baseball player in 1878.

Fowler was a skilled catcher, first baseman, and pitcher, but his best field position was second base. He was also great at hitting the ball, batting over .300 every season. (That means he reached base at least three times out of every ten times at bat.) Fowler was even a baseball innovator. Because so many white players were intentionally striking his legs with their spiked shoes, Fowler began wearing wooden slats over

his shins so he could protect himself—creating
the first baseball shin guards!

But as good as Fowler was on the field, no
baseball teams kept him on their roster for very
long. As soon as a good white player came along

who played the same position as Fowler, he would be fired. By the time he stopped playing baseball, Fowler had suited up for more than fourteen different teams in nine different leagues over ten years.

Another important black player in pro baseball's early days was a man named Moses Walker. In 1884, Walker joined the all-white Toledo Blue Stockings—the first black man to play on a major-league team.

Walker was a catcher. Part of his job was to tell the pitcher what type of ball to throw to each player. But one of the pitchers on his team refused to take orders from a black player. No matter how many hand signals Walker would give, the pitcher always ignored him.

As other black players tried to join white baseball clubs, professional baseball leagues all across the country worked together to stop this from happening. There was an unwritten

Moses Walker with the Toledo Blue Stockings, 1884

agreement: No black players would be hired. And indeed, none were. By 1899, black players were totally shut out of professional baseball.

But these black players did not give up. As famed civil rights activist Dr. W. E. B. Du Bois said, "If Negroes were to survive and prosper in White America they would have to do for themselves what whites were unwilling to do." These black players decided that if they couldn't play on white teams, then they would create their own.

CHAPTER 2
The First Black Pro Teams

In 1885, Frank P. Thompson was a headwaiter at the Argyle Hotel, a resort on Long Island, New York. According to black baseball player and historian Sol White, Thompson noticed that a number of the waiters at the hotel played baseball in their free time. Thompson hired these men and others to form the first professional black baseball team. They were called the Cuban Giants.

Original Cuban Giants, 1885

Why did they call themselves "Cubans"?

According to Sol White, who actually played for the Giants in 1891, it was to hide the fact of being black. (They also supposedly spoke a made-up language on the field that sounded like Spanish.) It's possible that the team thought they would face less racism by pretending to be Hispanic.

In time, the name "Giants" began to serve as a code word to let African American baseball fans know that a team was made up of black players. Other black teams started to pop up across the United States, with names like the Elite Giants, the Leland Giants, and the Mohawk Giants.

As good as these teams were, their fan base wasn't nearly as big as that of the white professional teams. The teams could not make enough money from the number of tickets bought by local fans. So they had to go on the road. Teams like the Cuban Giants often had to travel long distances for weeks or months to find teams to play against and new fans who would pay to watch the games.

Barnstorming, as it was called, became the way of life for black baseball players. The teams would load up all their players and equipment in buses or cars and travel from town to town,

looking for other baseball clubs to play. To make as much money as possible, they often scheduled two or three games in a single day (doubleheaders and triple-headers). The Homestead Grays were reported to travel thirty thousand miles during a 179-game season. In the cold winter months, many teams traveled to the Caribbean and Central or South America so they could continue playing.

Barnstorming was hardest when black ball teams traveled through the southern United States.

In 1896, the United States Supreme Court upheld a law. It said that segregation was legal.

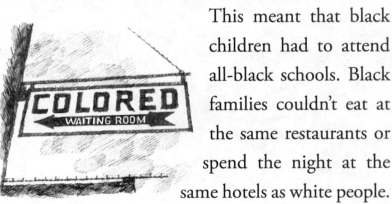

This meant that black children had to attend all-black schools. Black families couldn't eat at the same restaurants or spend the night at the same hotels as white people.

They couldn't even use the same bathrooms as white people or drink from the same water fountains—and the restrooms for black people were never as nice. Many times, black players had to sleep in people's homes if there wasn't a hotel for black people in town. Other times, they would sleep on the ground next to the baseball field.

Even so, black baseball players loved the game so much that they kept on going. They played anywhere, against anyone, anytime!

What Black Players Were Paid

The salaries for the Cuban Giants at the end of the 1800s were $18 a week for pitchers and catchers, $15 for infielders, and $12 for outfielders.

The travel schedule of a black baseball team, the Newark Eagles, in 1939:

Saturday: Game in Wilmington, Delaware, then travel on to Baltimore, Maryland.

Sunday: Doubleheader in Richmond, Virginia, then travel back to Baltimore.

Monday: Travel to Bellefonte, Pennsylvania.

Tuesday: Buffalo, New York

Wednesday: Pittsburgh, Pennsylvania

Thursday: Altoona, Pennsylvania

Friday: Canton, New York

Saturday: Pittsburgh

Sunday: Indianapolis, Indiana (doubleheader)

Tuesday: Akron, Ohio, return trip to Newark, New Jersey.

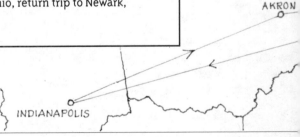

AKRON

INDIANAPOLIS

This may not seem like a lot of money, but it was a good salary compared with the wages for most black laborers. Still, black baseball players only made a fraction of what white players earned.

For the Cuban Giants, that meant playing twice as many games for half as much money.

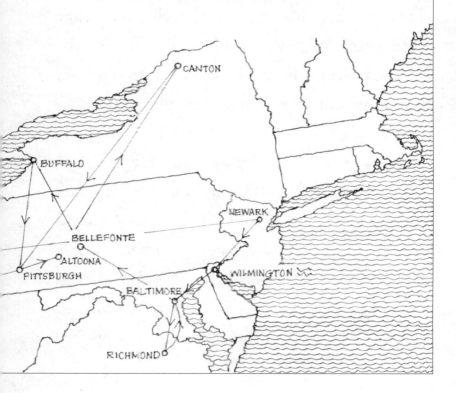

CHAPTER 3
Early Black Baseball Stars

Even though black players weren't allowed to play *on* white teams, at times they played *against* white teams. This gave black players a chance to show how good they really were—like when Frank Wickware, a black pitcher with the Mohawk Giants, beat a white barnstorming team by striking out seventeen of their players.

John Henry "Pop" Lloyd

Another star of this early era was John Henry "Pop" Lloyd. Some people called him "the black Honus Wagner." Other people thought Pop Lloyd was even *better* than Wagner, the white shortstop for the Pittsburgh Pirates. In 1911, when he was twenty-seven years old, Pop Lloyd hit 0.475 against semipro players. He continued to be a strong hitter throughout his career. In 1928, at forty-four years old, he hit 0.458!

Pop played some of his best baseball against white teams with star players such as Ty Cobb. Cobb, who mostly played for the Detroit Tigers, was the American League batting champion for nine consecutive years from 1907 to 1915. In 1911, he led the league in every major offensive category except home runs.

Ty Cobb may have been a *great* baseball player, but he wasn't a *nice* baseball player. Not only was he racist, he was despised by other baseball players— including his teammates.

Ty Cobb

Honus Wagner (1874–1955)

At the turn of the 1900s, John Peter "Honus" Wagner was the most dominant player in the major leagues. Hall of Fame player and manager John McGraw called Wagner "the nearest thing to a perfect player." He was a complete player, having played every position except catcher in the major leagues. In 1936, he was one of the first five players inducted into the Baseball Hall of Fame.

But as famous as Wagner is for his skill on the  field, he may be even more famous due to his baseball card. By some estimates, only fifty of Wagner's baseball cards were ever distributed. In October 2016, one of these rare cards sold for over $3 million!

When Cobb died in 1961, only four people from baseball attended his funeral.

In November 1910, Pop and Cobb faced off for a series of games in Havana, Cuba. As a shortstop, part of Pop's job was to protect second base. Cobb was one of the best in the game at *stealing* second base.

Ty Cobb tried to steal second base three times during the series. Pop stopped him each time.

Pop Lloyd was just as good at swinging the bat during the Havana series. He batted .500, the best of all the players—black and white. Cobb came in fourth with a batting average of .369. Supposedly, Ty Cobb was so mad at being shown up by a black baseball team that he vowed to never play against black players again.

Another star of black baseball in the early 1900s was Louis Santop of the Hilldale team. He was one of the first great black sluggers. Because of the way he could knock a ball out of the field, his nickname was "Big Bertha," after a huge World War I German weapon that could fire a projectile almost six miles.

Big Bertha, 1914

Santop was often compared to Babe Ruth. They finally faced off against each other on October 12, 1920, in Shibe Park, Philadelphia. Babe Ruth batted four times, ending up with a walk, a fly-ball out, and two strikeouts. Santop had four at bats as well—and he ended up with a double and two singles. Santop's team won the game 5–0.

Andrew "Rube" Foster

One baseball player from this era would not only be known as a great player on the field, but also become one of the most important leaders in organized black baseball. His name was Andrew "Rube" Foster. He's often called "the Father of Black Baseball."

CHAPTER 4
The Father of Black Baseball

Andrew Foster was born on September 17, 1879, in Calvert, Texas. The son of a preacher, Foster attended church almost every Sunday while growing up. But Andrew also loved baseball and would often slip away to the baseball fields on

Sunday afternoon. He loved the game so much that he quit school after eighth grade and ran away from home to try his luck at becoming a professional baseball player.

By the time he was seventeen, Andrew was playing semiprofessional baseball for the Fort Worth Yellow Jackets. (Semiprofessional ballplayers are part-time players who earn a living through other work.) By 1902, he was playing professional baseball for the Cuban Giants of Philadelphia, Pennsylvania.

Andrew was a very confident player. He called himself the best pitcher in the country. He claimed to have won fifty-one games in 1902, including one against the all-white Philadelphia Athletics and their star player Rube Waddell. After that, Andrew's teammates began calling him "Rube."

Rube wasn't just a great pitcher. He was a power hitter, too. According to legend, he once hit a ball so hard that it fell apart in midair.

Rube was a baseball innovator, as well. He wanted the game to be played in new ways. He invented the "hit-and-run bunt." A bunt is when a hitter taps a ball instead of slugging it. If a fast runner was already on first base, a bunted ball rolling down the third baseline was almost impossible to defend. Even major-league managers would come out to Rube's games to study how he did it. And there's also a story where Rube was hired by the all-white New York Giants in 1903 to teach his screwball to their pitchers, including Hall of Famer Joe "Iron Man" McGinnity.

Like most black baseball players of that time, Rube switched from team to team, depending on the money offered. In 1903, Foster went from the Cuban Giants to the Cuban X-Giants (another black team made up of *ex*–Cuban Giants players). Just a year later, Rube took almost that entire team with him when he signed with the Philadelphia Giants.

As Rube neared the end of his playing career, he decided that he wanted to run a team. By 1911, he had partnered with a white business owner to form the Chicago American Giants. With Rube as manager, the team had much success.

Chicago American Giants, 1914

But, as always, there was trouble keeping it together. Teams from the East would try to "steal" Rube's star players by promising more money—sometimes more than they really had.

Now that he was a manager, Rube didn't want players jumping from team to team (even though he had done the same thing himself). But most black baseball teams acted independently of one another. They didn't get together to set rules that might forbid players from doing all this moving around.

Rube realized that there needed to be an organized league for black teams. Teams would have to agree to standard contracts that provided fair payment to players and barred teams from stealing rival players.

There had been attempts to form a black baseball league since 1886. But none lasted. One reason was lack of money. Leagues needed team owners who could pay for equipment, staff and players, and practice field rentals. There weren't many black business owners with enough money to do that. Those who did have the money often thought that investing in professional baseball was too risky.

But, eventually, Rube devised a plan to get black baseball teams and black businessmen to work together. This led to the birth of the Negro National League.

First Attempts at an All-Black Baseball League

One of the first attempts to form a black baseball league began in 1886. The League of Colored Baseball Clubs included eight teams located in cities such as New York, Boston, Philadelphia, and Pittsburgh. The league developed written rules and a way to evenly share the money. Unfortunately, the league struggled with financial problems and wasn't able to schedule games regularly. The League of Colored Baseball Clubs lasted only one week.

Another all-black league was formed in 1890. Its teams came from cities with large black populations— including Louisville, Kansas City, Chicago, and Cleveland. Still, this league failed as well. The teams struggled to raise money for equipment, and worried about losing money when they had to travel to other cities to play games.

CHAPTER 5
A League of Their Own

In 1919, Rube called together the owners of the most successful black teams in the Midwest, ones he knew would not go out of business. In February 1920, the owners met in Kansas City and formed the Negro National League (NNL). The league included seven black-owned teams, and one white-owned team.

Foster was elected the first president of the NNL. He created strict rules that would stop teams from "stealing" players. He also moved some players to different teams in order to create a balanced league, where a few teams wouldn't dominate all the others. This included sending his own star player, center fielder Oscar Charleston, to the Indianapolis ABCs.

Oscar Charleston

When teams ran out of money, Rube sent some so they could continue to travel and play. He even financed the Dayton Marcos baseball club from his own bank account.

But Rube couldn't just focus on the league— he also had his own team to run. And as the owner of the Chicago American Giants, he wanted his team to win!

Rube built his ball club for speed. The third baseman, Dave Malarcher, claimed that at least seven men in the lineup could run a hundred yards in ten seconds.

Bunting was just as important. During a game, after a player bunted and got on base, Rube would use his hitters, Jim Brown and Cristóbal Torriente, to bring players home.

Rube's style of baseball was exciting—full of players flying around the bases, stealing home, and balls bouncing across the field. His style also won games. The Chicago American Giants won the first three Negro National League pennants from 1920 to 1922.

The league was quickly becoming a success, as well. In 1920, the opening game between the Indianapolis ABCs and the Chicago American Giants drew a crowd of six thousand at Washington Park in Indianapolis. Three years later, on April 28, 1923, the ABCs brought in a

crowd of nine thousand for their season-opening game. The Giants and the Kansas City Monarchs drew in fifteen thousand people for a game in Chicago that same year. Overall, it's estimated that over four hundred thousand people attended league games in 1923.

Thanks to Foster, the Negro National League became one of the most successful black-owned businesses in the country. The teams in the league had spectacular baseball players that fans couldn't wait to see.

Bud Fowler (center back), the first African American to play on
an integrated professional team, 1885

Rube Foster of the Leland Giants, 1909

Rube Foster (front row, center) and John Henry "Pop" Lloyd
(back row, second from right) with the Chicago American Giants, 1914

A crowd watches the Cuban Giants during a barnstorming game, 1916.

Oscar Charleston, 1928

A baseball game at Greenlee Field, 1930s

James "Cool Papa" Bell of the Homestead Grays, 1932

The 1934 Kansas City Monarchs

Walter "Buck" Leonard of the Homestead Grays at bat,
Griffith Stadium, 1930s

The 1935 Pittsburgh Crawfords in front of their team bus

A segregated restaurant in the South, 1938

Satchel Paige of the Kansas City Monarchs and Josh Gibson
of the Homestead Grays, 1940s

Gus Greenlee's restaurant, the Crawford Grill, 1950s

Gus Greenlee at the Crawford Grill, 1945

Pitcher Satchel Paige winds up, 1941.

Josh Gibson is tagged out during the East-West Game, 1944.

Branch Rickey watches Jackie Robinson sign with
the Brooklyn Dodgers, 1947.

Jackie Robinson slides toward home plate, 1948.

Jackie Robinson signs autographs, 1948.

One of the last Negro American League teams,
the Birmingham Black Barons, 1951

Former Negro League players in their major-league uniforms
(from left to right: Jackie Robinson, George Crowe, Joe Black,
Sam Jethroe, Roy Campanella, and Bill Bruton), 1952

Jackie Robinson and Dodgers teammate Pee Wee Reese, 1952

James "Cool Papa" Bell holds a photo of his Hall of Fame plaque, 1990.

The Negro Leagues Baseball Museum in Kansas City, 2013

CHAPTER 6
The Negro Leagues Grow

Due to the Negro National League's early success, other team owners in different parts of the country were eager to create their own all-black baseball leagues. A few months after the founding of the NNL, seven Southern-based ball clubs formed the Negro Southern League (NSL). The NSL developed a 104-game schedule, and established player and salary limits for each team. Although the NSL broke into smaller leagues after the 1921 season, these new leagues kept a similar structure.

In December 1922, six ball clubs in the

Northeast started the Eastern Colored League (ECL). The ECL immediately began to raid players from the NNL, including star catcher James "Biz" Mackey, and the American Giants' own pitcher, Dave Brown. These actions angered Foster so much that he threatened a lifetime ban for any NNL players who joined the ECL. He

also refused to play against the ECL in a World Series at the end of the season.

However, by the end of the 1924 season, Foster agreed to support a World Series between the NNL's Kansas City Monarchs and the ECL's Hilldale after the two leagues agreed to respect each other's player contracts.

Negro Leagues World Series, 1924

The Monarchs won the first game of the series by a score of 6–2, but Hilldale came back 11–0 to win the second game. After three additional wins by each team and a tie, both teams came into the deciding tenth game needing a win in order to claim the championship.

The Hilldale starting pitcher was Holsey "Scrip" Lee. Lee's unusual "submarine" pitching style—where he released the ball close to the ground—was difficult for many players to hit.

For the first seven innings, Hilldale's Lee dominated the game, not allowing any runs and only giving up one hit.

Things finally turned for the Monarchs in the eighth, when the team scored five runs. The Monarchs won 5–0, claiming the 1924 World Series. But the real hero of the game was José Méndez, who threw a three-hitter and didn't allow a single Hilldale runner to reach second base. And Rube Foster was right there in the dugout, sending pitching signals to Méndez from the bench.

Even with all of Foster's success, the stress of running the league was wearing on him. He was reported to be seen chasing imaginary fly balls outside of his Chicago home. Bobby Williams, Foster's shortstop, once claimed that Rube tried to lock himself in a bathroom and refused to open the door. Another player had to climb on top of the roof and through a window to get him out.

In 1926, Rube had to give up control of both his team and his league, and he was sent to a hospital for mentally ill patients. But even without Rube in charge, his NNL continued on, bringing fans to the sport—and making money for owners, managers, and players.

Then, in October 1929, the stock market crashed. That led to the Great Depression. People lost their homes and their jobs. Banks closed, leaving many people without money. Farmers couldn't afford to harvest their crops, creating more huge shortages.

Rube Foster's Later Life

Sadly, Rube spent the rest of his life at the hospital, dying on December 9, 1930. He had a huge funeral, with over three thousand mourners standing outside of the church as his casket was carried out. Even in death, Rube Foster brought a crowd.

Baseball, too, was hit hard by the Depression. People couldn't afford tickets to games anymore. The ECL, now reorganized as the Negro American League, folded at the end of the 1929 season. Rube's Negro National League folded in 1931. By the end of 1932, almost all professional black baseball leagues had folded. Most teams survived as they had before the NNL—as independent teams barnstorming and playing against anyone in order to make a little money.

However, there were a few people with enough power—and money—who wanted to keep organized black baseball afloat. They had seen the benefits of the Negro National League and wanted to bring it back again.

CHAPTER 7
The Second Negro National League

Gus Greenlee

A black man named Gus Greenlee helped carry on what Rube Foster had started.

Greenlee had been a small-time criminal in 1920s Pittsburgh—making and selling liquor, which was illegal then in the United States, and gambling. However, he also became the successful owner of two hotels and a popular restaurant named the Crawford Grill. And over time, Greenlee helped out the black community in Pittsburgh. He gave money to

the National Association for the Advancement of Colored People (NAACP), a national group that fought for equal rights for black people. He gave food to needy families every Christmas.

By 1931, he began to finance the Pittsburgh Crawfords, a semipro team that played on a sandlot near his restaurant. The following year, he hired professional players to join the team.

He even helped to finance a new field, Greenlee Field, for his new team. It was the first stadium ever built for a black team. It cost around $100,000—that would be $1.7 million in today's

Pittsburgh Crawfords in Greenlee Field

economy. In 1932 alone, almost seventy thousand fans attended baseball games at Greenlee Field.

While most black residents of Pittsburgh cheered on their new baseball team, others weren't

so happy—especially Cum Posey. He was the owner of the other "local" team, the Homestead Grays.

Cumberland "Cum" Posey was born in 1890 in Homestead, Pennsylvania. The town was

Cumberland "Cum" Posey

only seven miles from downtown Pittsburgh. Posey was also black, but, unlike Greenlee, he came from a wealthy family and had a college education. But, like Greenlee, Posey also believed in giving back to the black community. He served as a member of the local board of education for fifteen years. He also helped raise money for sports and sports facilities for local youth.

In 1911, Posey joined a black team called the
Homestead Grays. He was a decent player. But
he was more successful later as a manager and an
owner. Posey built the Grays into a powerhouse
team, playing—and defeating—most other black
baseball teams. In 1931, they won over 130 games
and lost only 10.

Unfortunately, the Depression hit the Grays hard. In 1932, the Grays made less money than they had in any of the past twenty years. Greenlee, too, found that owning the Crawfords during the Great Depression came at a steep cost.

Because the two teams were located so near each other, it would have made sense for them to play against each other. However, Posey really disliked Greenlee. He refused to let his team play against the Crawfords.

People, however, were willing to pay money to see these two top teams square off. So Posey looked past his dislike for Greenlee, and the two teams began playing against each other.

After the 1932 season, Greenlee began to reconsider barnstorming. Instead of primarily playing baseball on the road, he wanted to bring more games—and revenue—to his new stadium. So in 1933, he called together black baseball owners and formed a new Negro National League.

Greenlee thought up different ways to get fans excited about the league, including creating the East-West Game. Modeled after Major League Baseball's All-Star Game, the East-West game featured  the best players in black baseball. Players were selected through fan voting in two major black newspapers. The East-West Game became a huge success for the league, with attendance regularly exceeding over fifty thousand people.

The new Negro National League was a major victory for organized black baseball.

CHAPTER 8
The Crawfords and the Grays

Why had Cum Posey disliked Gus Greenlee for such a long time?

The reason was simple.

Before the creation of the Negro National League, Greenlee had stolen the top players from Cum Posey's roster. In all, Greenlee "stole" away eight players—including future Hall of Famers Oscar Charleston and Josh Gibson.

When describing Oscar Charleston, another Negro League player once said, "He was like [Hall of Famers] Ty Cobb, Babe Ruth, and Tris Speaker rolled into one." Born in 1896, Charleston played center field for some of the best teams in black baseball, including the Indianapolis ABCs, Foster's American Giants in Chicago, and the Saint Louis Giants. While playing for the Saint Louis Giants in 1921, Charleston batted .434, and led the team in doubles, home runs, and stolen bases.

At age thirty-five, Charleston was long past his prime by the time he joined the Crawfords in 1932. But Charleston still had a sharp baseball mind. Greenlee had Charleston serve as both a player and a manager.

Slugger Josh Gibson was born in 1911 in Buena Vista, Georgia. His parents were originally sharecroppers, but by 1924, his father had found work in a steel plant in Pittsburgh. By the age of sixteen, Gibson had dropped out of school and was playing baseball for an all-black amateur team. He joined the Homestead Grays in July of 1930. The following year, he knocked in seventy-five home runs for the team . . . and then Greenlee lured him over to the Crawfords.

Greenlee didn't just look to the rival Grays for talent. In 1933, Greenlee hired James "Cool Papa" Bell away from the Saint Louis Stars.

Born in 1903, Bell played baseball for twenty-five years, until 1947. His best year was in 1933, when he stole 175 bases. Bell was rumored to be fast enough to make it from first base to third on a bunt. Another famous story was that Bell was so quick, he could flip off a light switch and be in the bed before the room became dark.

Perhaps Greenlee's smartest move came in 1931, when he purchased the contract of Satchel Paige from the Cleveland Cubs. Satchel is often considered the best pitcher in Negro League history. He not only wowed audiences with his fastball, but also with his showmanship. One time he pitched with no other players from his team on the field. He said he was "Satchel Paige, World's Greatest Pitcher, Guaranteed to Strike Out the First Nine Men." He sometimes arrived late to the game with a police escort—just so he could make a grand entrance. Satchel would also routinely show off by placing a gum wrapper on home plate, and then repeatedly firing fastballs directly over it to show off his speed and accuracy.

Satchel had a number of nicknames for his pitches. He called his fastball Long Tom, or bee ball (because it flew so fast that it hummed). His other special pitches included his looper, nothing ball, bat dodger, hurry-up ball, midnight rider, and the four-day creeper.

In 1935, Greenlee's Crawfords defeated the New York Cubans in a seven-game series to win the NNL championship. But by 1937, the Crawfords' growing payroll, the cost of running a league, and his own troubles with the law soon caught up with him. After Greenlee sold the club in 1939, he had to stand by and watch Cum Posey's Homestead Grays dominate the NNL.

Thanks to the hitting of first baseman Walter "Buck" Leonard and Josh Gibson (whom Greenlee was forced to trade back to the Grays), the Homestead Grays won their first NNL pennant in 1937. They would win eight more pennants over the next eleven seasons.

In 1937, a rival league, a new Negro American League (NAL), began its first season. The NAL featured eight teams, including the Kansas City Monarchs. The two leagues faced off in a World Series in 1942. And while the Grays could easily claim to be the best team in the NNL, it was the Kansas City Monarchs—now led by Satchel Paige—who won the 1942 Negro Leagues World Series.

Three years later, the Monarchs would pick up a talented young player who had recently been released from the army. His name was Jackie Robinson, and he would change the course of both Major League Baseball and Negro League Baseball forever.

Jackie Robinson

CHAPTER 9
The Great Experiment

In the early 1900s, long before Jackie Robinson began his baseball career, a man named Wesley Branch Rickey served as a baseball coach for a small college in Ohio. The team's catcher was named Charles Thomas. He was the only black player on the team.

Wesley Branch Rickey

One day, while on a road trip, Thomas was refused a hotel room. Years later, Rickey said that the tall young pitcher had cried while he looked at his hands and said, "Black skin . . . black skin. If only I could make 'em white." The encounter made a lasting impression on Rickey.

Kansas City Monarchs

J. L. Wilkinson

J. L. Wilkinson, who was a white man, formed the Kansas City Monarchs in 1920. They quickly became one of the best teams in the Midwest, winning ten pennants as members of the first Negro National League and the Negro American League. Wilkinson's rosters included Hall of Famers Cool Papa Bell, Satchel Paige, and Jackie Robinson.

Monarchs baseball player and manager Newt Allen called Wilkinson "one of the best owners ever" in Negro League Baseball. Bill Drake, a pitcher for the Monarchs, called the team "the Yankees of Negro baseball."

Charles Thomas

Branch Rickey would go on to play professional baseball for a few years before becoming a lawyer. Later, he returned to the sport, in time becoming general manager for the Saint Louis Cardinals.

Rickey soon realized how hard it was to get good players, because other teams with more money could offer better contracts than the Cardinals could. Rickey wanted to create a system where he could find young new talent, bring them into the Cardinals organization, and help them grow into first-rate players. Eventually, he developed minor-league teams. Called "farm teams," they acted as training grounds for the major leagues.

The system worked just like Rickey thought it would. From 1930 to 1934, Rickey's "farm team" talent would lead the Cardinals to win three pennants and two World Series.

Dodgers

In 1942, Branch Rickey moved from Missouri to New York, where he became the president and general manager for the Brooklyn Dodgers. The Dodgers were a disappointment compared to the other New York baseball teams, the Yankees and the Giants. Those teams had won a combined thirteen World Series by 1940. The Dodgers finally made it to the World Series in 1941 . . . only to lose the series 4–1 to the Yankees. In addition, the Dodgers spent most of the 1930s in debt.

However, Branch Rickey had a startling idea for how to quickly turn the lovable losers into a winning and profitable team. Rickey believed that it was time for Major League Baseball to hire black players. Other sports, such as boxing, were already integrated.

Rickey felt sure that black players would

African American boxing champion Joe Louis knocks out
his opponent, Billy Conn, 1941

bring more fans to games. African Americans
had proved what enthusiastic baseball fans they
were. They attended Negro League games in huge
numbers. He bet that both black and white fans
would pay to see them play. But more than making
money, Branch Rickey wanted a championship
team. He knew how exciting and talented black
baseball players were. When speaking about his
reasons for integrating baseball, Rickey would
later say, "I simply wanted to win a pennant for
the Brooklyn Dodgers, and I wanted the best

human beings I could find to help me win it."
Luck was on Rickey's side in his quest to
hire black players. In 1945,
A. B. "Happy" Chandler became
the new commissioner of Major
League Baseball. Unlike the last
commissioner, Chandler was
open to allowing black
players into the league.

Branch Rickey began
to quietly scout black

A.B. "Happy" Chandler

players. He wasn't just looking for the best athlete
to join his club. He was looking for a certain
type of player. He needed a player who could
remain calm when men on opposing teams yelled
at him. He needed a player who would choose
not to fight back even if another player tried to
hurt him on the field.

In 1945, he found the perfect man for the job.

CHAPTER 10
Jackie Robinson

Jack Roosevelt Robinson was born in Georgia in January 1919, the youngest of five children. After the family moved to California, his mother worked hard to provide for her children, taking a job as a cook and maid in Pasadena.

Jackie attended the University of California, Los Angeles, where he excelled in four sports. He even played semipro football for a short while. But after the United States entered World War II at the end of 1941, he joined the army.

In April 1942, Jackie attended Officer Candidate School at Fort Riley, Kansas. His class was the first to include black and white soldiers. After graduation, he became a second lieutenant and was sent to Fort Hood, Texas. Even though he was now an officer, he was forced to live and eat separately from white officers.

On July 6, 1944, a bus driver ordered Jackie to move to the back of a military bus. The front of the bus had been reserved for white passengers only. Jackie refused to move. He was arrested and given a court-martial—a military trial. If the judge found him guilty, Jackie could be sent to jail— maybe for a long time. During the trial, Jackie defended himself. The bus driver had no right to order him to move or call him names. At the end of the four-hour trial, Jackie was cleared of any wrongdoing.

Jackie was then stationed in Kentucky, where he met a soldier who had played in the Negro Leagues. The idea of playing sports for a living appealed to Jackie. So in 1945, less than a year after leaving the army, he joined the Kansas City Monarchs.

Jackie had trouble adjusting to the "freewheeling" nature of the Negro League at first. His teammate, Satchel Paige, was still the master showman. Paige often played for only two or three innings of a game before leaving the stadium to join an all-star team. Jackie didn't approve of that. Jackie also didn't like the long bus rides, and the racism he faced while on the road.

Once, the Kansas City Monarchs stopped at a gas station in Oklahoma to fill up on gas.

However, the attendant selling the gas wouldn't let the team use the bathroom. After Jackie threatened to buy gas somewhere else, the attendant gave in. From then on, the team never bought gas anywhere they weren't also allowed to use the bathroom.

As far as his playing, Jackie had a good year. He finished the season with a .345 batting average in forty-one games. He was also voted the starting shortstop for the West in the annual East-West Game.

Branch Rickey began to study Jackie closer, and he liked what he saw—both on the field and off. After meeting with Jackie in the summer of 1945, Rickey signed Jackie to a major-league contract!

First, Jackie would play for the Montreal Royals, the Dodgers' minor-league team. After time there, he would make his major-league debut.

Rickey tried to keep his plans a secret. In order to fool other major-league baseball teams, Rickey first announced that the Dodgers were thinking about starting their own black baseball club. That was why he met with players like Jackie Robinson.

But other major-league teams discovered Rickey's plans, and they were not happy. They voted 15–1 to bar Jackie from entering the league. However, Commissioner Chandler overturned the vote and approved the deal.

Just as Rickey thought, Jackie faced many obstacles in his first year playing in the minor leagues. During spring training, Jackie was forced to eat and sleep separately from his white teammates. Once, a game against the Royals was canceled. The excuse was that the lights didn't work—although it was an afternoon contest!

Even the Royals' own manager called Jackie names, claiming that Jackie wasn't a real human because he was black.

Jackie kept quiet when people taunted him. He let his playing speak for him. He helped lead the Royals to the minor-league World Series.

Branch Rickey saw everything he needed to see. The following year, on April 15, 1947, Jackie took the field for the Brooklyn Dodgers.

On that day, he became the first black player to play Major League Baseball in modern times.

It was a special day—not just for Jackie. Over half of the twenty-six thousand fans at the stadium that day were black. Many of the black men wore coats and ties. Black women wore fancy scarves and gloves. These were not normal clothes for a day at the ballpark. These black families had dressed in their "Sunday best" in honor of Jackie Robinson.

Jackie smiled as he took the field at first base. When he caught a pass from the third baseman to score the game's first out, the crowd cheered for him. They roared even louder when he took his first at bat. Jackie would finally score in the seventh inning, putting the team up 4–3. The Dodgers went on to win their first game.

The *Pittsburgh Courier*, 1947

Black-owned newspapers all over the country reported about Jackie. The *Pittsburgh Courier* devoted most of its first page to Jackie. The *Boston Chronicle* proclaimed "Triumph of Whole Race Seen in Jackie's Debut in Major League Baseball."

Jackie's first year in the majors was hard. Fans booed and threw garbage at him. Pitches were thrown directly at his head. Some of his own teammates signed a petition saying that they didn't want him on the team. Once team manager Leo Durocher learned of the petition, he called a team meeting and said, "I don't care if he is yellow or black or has stripes . . . I'm his manager and I say he plays."

During Jackie's first series against the Phillies, the opposing team's manager and players called him names and told him to "go back to the cotton fields." But instead of Jackie talking back, it was

Eddie Stanky and Jackie Robinson

teammate Eddie Stanky, one of the men who had signed the petition, who stood up for Jackie. He said, "Why don't you yell at someone who can answer back?" While playing against another very nasty team, Dodgers team captain Harold "Pee Wee" Reese called a time-out, put his hand on Jackie's shoulder, and offered words of encouragement. Slowly, Jackie was becoming a member of the team.

Jackie ended the season batting .297 with twenty-nine stolen bases and twelve home runs. He was elected Rookie of the Year by the *Sporting News* magazine.

One of Jackie's best seasons came in 1949, when he led the league in hitting and was named the National League Most Valuable Player.

MVP Award

Jackie would continue to play for the Dodgers until he retired, helping them win the World Series in 1955. He was inducted into the Baseball Hall of Fame in 1962.

Branch Rickey's "great experiment" had worked—first for Jackie and the Dodgers, and then for every other black kid who dreamed about the major leagues. Baseball would never be the same.

CHAPTER 11
The End of an Era

Jackie Robinson changed Major League Baseball forever. He also changed the fate of the Negro Leagues. Other black players followed Jackie to the majors in quick succession.

In 1946, black catcher Roy Campanella joined Jackie Robinson in the Dodgers farm system.

A year later, Larry Doby joined the Cleveland Indians. Soon, all major-league teams were scouting black baseball players—though it took until 1959 for every MLB club to have at least one black player on its roster.

As fans of black baseball now flocked to watch their heroes play in the majors, attendance at NNL games fell. In 1947, only two NNL teams made a profit. A year later, in 1948, the once-mighty Negro National League folded.

Roy Campanella (left)
with Jackie Robinson

The Negro American League struggled, too, with many of its teams returning to barnstorming. The last NAL club, the Birmingham Black Barons, folded in 1960.

The Negro League era was over.

Veteran Negro League players, managers, and owners had mixed feelings about Jackie Robinson breaking Major League Baseball's color barrier. Most were thrilled, even at the expense of their league. Others were probably understandably upset because some Negro League greats—early stars such as Pop Lloyd and Oscar Charleston, and giants like Josh Gibson and Cool Papa Bell— never got a spot on a major-league team due to their age and health.

But there were a few aging Negro League stars still determined to make it into the majors. One was Satchel Paige. His fastball wasn't as speedy, and his walk was a little slower, but his arm was still good enough to compete.

And that's how, on July 9, 1948, Satchel Paige became the oldest rookie in MLB history when he took the field for the Cleveland Indians. He was thirty-nine.

CHAPTER 12
Their Place in History

On July 25, 1966, power hitter Ted Williams was inducted into the National Baseball Hall of Fame. During the ceremony, he stated, "I hope someday Satchel Paige and Josh Gibson will be voted into the Hall of Fame as symbols of the great Negro players who are not here only because they weren't given the chance."

Ted Williams during his Baseball Hall of Fame induction, 1966

Williams's statement was groundbreaking. It got people within baseball talking—and moving.

In 1971, Satchel Paige was elected to the Hall of Fame. Yes, he had played briefly in the majors,

but he was being honored for his days on Negro League teams. Satchel's teammate, Josh Gibson, joined him in 1972. (Jackie Robinson had been inducted years before them in 1962, but he had spent his career almost entirely in the major leagues.)

Today, thirty-five players and executives in the Baseball Hall of Fame spent most of their careers with Negro League Baseball.

Maybe the most important induction took place in 1981. Sixty-one years after the formation

of his Negro National League, Rube Foster, the Father of Black Baseball, took his rightful place among other baseball legends.

The Negro League era of baseball was over, but now it is forever enshrined as an important part of the history of the sport that is known as "America's pastime."

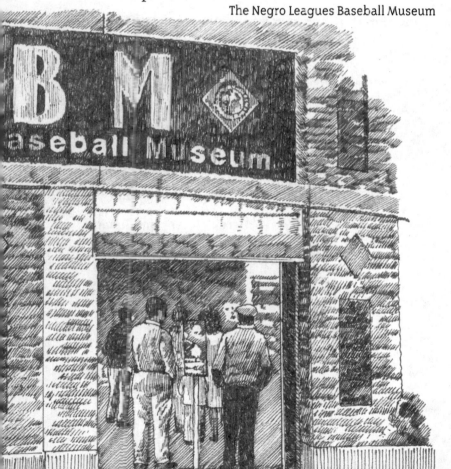

The Negro Leagues Baseball Museum

Diversity in Baseball

In 2018, 41 percent of Major League Baseball players were black, Latino, Asian, or came from other nonwhite cultures.

However, MLB still has much to improve with senior staff and ownership. The 2018 MLB season began with only four managers of color—Alex Cora of the Boston Red Sox, Dave Roberts of the Los Angeles Dodgers, Dave Martinez of the Washington Nationals, and Rick Rentería of the Chicago White Sox. And while sports stars like Derek Jeter and Magic Johnson are part owners of baseball teams, only one person of color, Arturo Moreno, is the majority owner of a ball club.

Derek Jeter

Magic Johnson

Major League Baseball has made great strides toward inclusion and diversity, but it's evident that the sport still has a long way to go.

Negro League Hall of Famers

Here is a list of Hall of Famers who spent all or most of their career in the Negro Leagues.

NAME	INDUCTION YEAR
James Thomas "Cool Papa" Bell	1974
Ray Brown	2006
Willard Brown	2006
Oscar Charleston	1976
Andy Cooper	2006
Ray Dandridge	1987
Leon Day	1995
Martín Dihigo	1977
Andrew "Rube" Foster	1981
Bill Foster	1996
Josh Gibson	1972
Ulysses Franklin "Frank" Grant	2006
Pete Hill	2006
Monte Irvin	1973
William Julius "Judy" Johnson	1975
Walter "Buck" Leonard	1972
John Henry "Pop" Lloyd	1977

NAME	INDUCTION YEAR
James Raleigh "Biz" Mackey	2006
Effa Manley	2006
José Méndez	2006
Leroy Robert "Satchel" Paige	1971
Alejandro "Alex" Pompez	2006
Cumberland "Cum" Posey	2006
Wilber Joe "Bullet" Rogan	1998
Louis Santop	2006
Hilton Smith	2001
Norman Thomas "Turkey" Stearnes	2000
George "Mule" Suttles	2006
Ben Taylor	2006
Cristóbal Torriente	2006
Willie Wells	1997
Sol White	2006
James Leslie "J. L." Wilkinson	2006
Joe Williams	1999
Ernest Judson "Jud" Wilson	2006

Timeline of the Negro Leagues

1865 — Civil War ends

— Thirteenth Amendment is passed, ending slavery

1869 — The Cincinnati Red Stockings become the first professional baseball team

1878 — Bud Fowler becomes the first black professional baseball player

1899 — Professional white baseball teams are no longer hiring black players

1920 — Andrew "Rube" Foster forms the first Negro National League

1931 — The Negro National League folds

1933 — Gus Greenlee organizes the second Negro National League

1945 — Jackie Robinson joins the Kansas City Monarchs

1947 — Jackie Robinson plays his first game for the Brooklyn Dodgers, becoming the first black player to play Major League Baseball in modern times

1948 — Satchel Paige makes his major-league debut for the Cleveland Indians

— The second Negro National League folds

1959 — Every Major League Baseball team has at least one black player on its roster

1960 — The Negro Leagues era ends

Timeline of the World

1865 — President Abraham Lincoln is killed

1869 — Mahatma Gandhi is born in India

1872 — The Metropolitan Museum of Art opens to the public in New York City

1920 — The Nineteenth Amendment gives women the right to vote

1929 — The stock market crashes

1931 — Construction begins on the Hoover Dam

1933 — Franklin D. Roosevelt is inaugurated as the thirty-second president of the United States

1936 — Jesse Owens wins four gold medals at the Olympic Games in Berlin

1941 — The United States enters World War II

1945 — World War II ends

1947 — *The Diary of a Young Girl* by Anne Frank is published

1948 — The US military ends segregation

1959 — Alaska and Hawaii become the forty-ninth and fiftieth states

1963 — Martin Luther King Jr. delivers his "I Have a Dream" speech during the March on Washington

1969 — American astronauts Neil Armstrong and Buzz Aldrin are the first people to land on the moon

Bibliography

*Books for young readers

Bankes, James. *The Pittsburgh Crawfords*. Jefferson, NC: McFarland & Co., 2001.

Eig, Jonathan. *Opening Day: The Story of Jackie Robinson's First Season*. New York: Simon & Schuster, 2007.

Hauser, Christopher. *The Negro Leagues Chronology: Events in Organized Black Baseball, 1920–1948*. Jefferson, NC: McFarland & Co., 2008.

Heaphy, Leslie A. *The Negro Leagues, 1869–1960*. Jefferson, NC: McFarland & Co., 2003.

*Herman, Gail. *Who Was Jackie Robinson?* New York: Penguin Workshop, 2011.

Holway, John. *Blackball Stars: Negro League Pioneers*. New York: Carroll & Graff Publishers, 1992.

Lanctot, Neil. *Negro League Baseball: The Rise and Ruin of a Black Institution*. Philadelphia: University of Pennsylvania Press, 2004.

*Nelson, Kadir. *We Are the Ship: The Story of Negro League Baseball*. New York: Jump at the Sun/Hyperion Books for Children, 2008.

*Ward, Geoffrey C., et al. *Shadow Ball: A History of the Negro Leagues*. New York: Knopf, 1994.